This book belongs to:

____

Also by *Nurse Dean*

A-Z For the Little Nurse In Me
A-Z For the Little Animal Lover In Me

A to Z

FOR THE LITTLE STOCK INVE$TOR IN ME

Barry Bedford Books Publication Company

BARRY BEDFORD BOOKS
A PUBLICATION COMPANY

– For my daughter Mila.

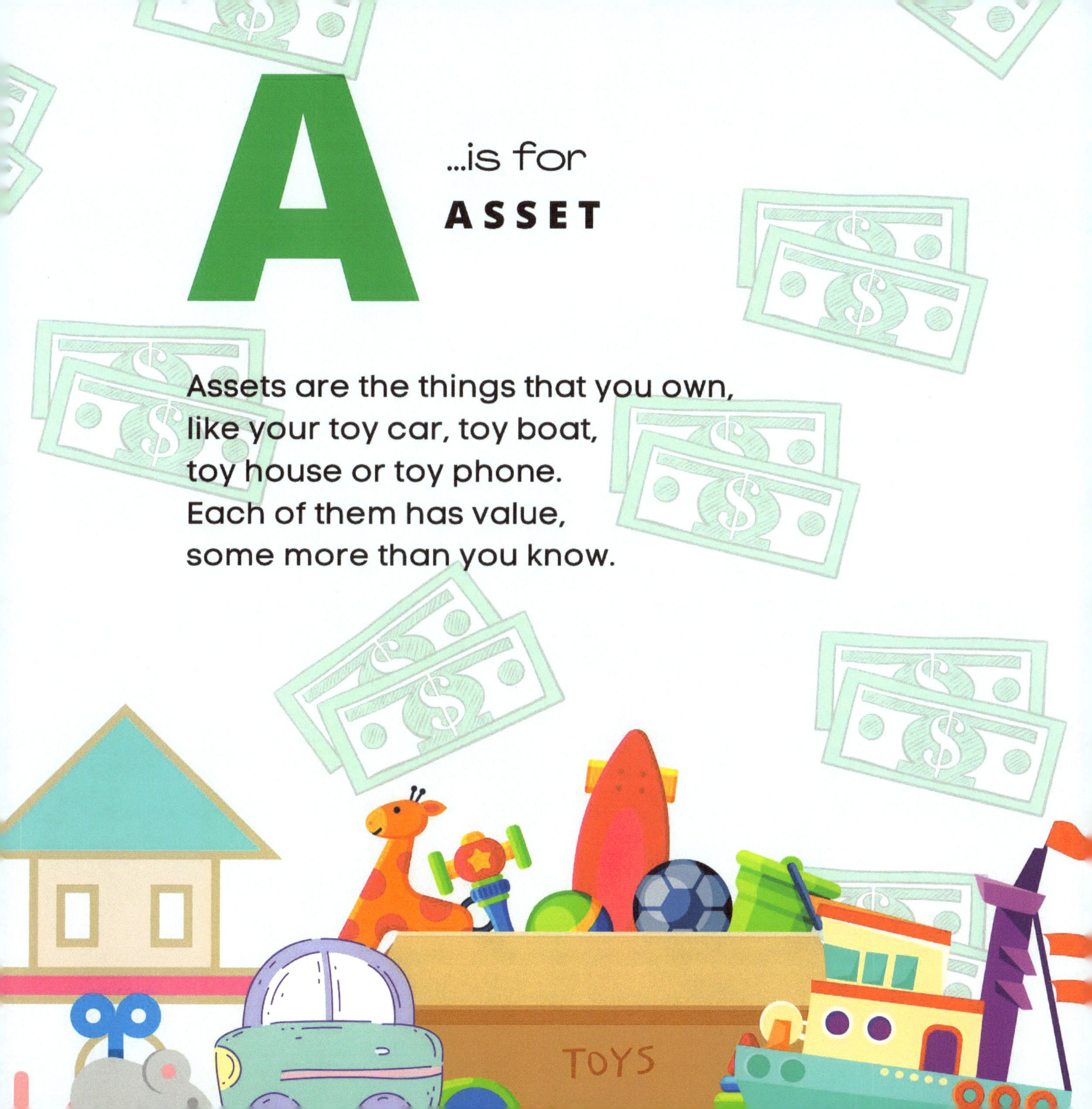

A

...is for

ASSET

Assets are the things that you own,
like your toy car, toy boat,
toy house or toy phone.
Each of them has value,
some more than you know.

B
...is for
BULLISH
If you think the price of a stock will rise
like birds that soar high in the sky
you're bullish on the stock !

C
...is for
CALL
OPTION
You can buy shares
or you can buy options.
If you think the price of a stock will fly
like a space rocket
then you should buy a call option!

D
...is for
DIVIDEND
Some companies pay you
for just owning a share.
If the dividend is 1 dollar
and you have 5 shares,
your dividend pay is 5 dollars
just for owning 5 shares
$5·00

...is for

EQUITY

You bought a toy train for
5 dollars and kept it nice and clean.

Then found out from a friend
your toy trains new dollar value is 15.

The difference is
10 dollars and that's your equity !

F

...is for

F.A.A.N.G.

The top 5 technology companies in the
stock market are
Facebook, Apple, Amazon,
Netflix and Google.
Together they are worth
oOdlEss and OooOdles !

G

...is for
GREEKS

If you want to buy options
these are the people you should know;
Delta, Vega, Theta,
Gamma, and Ro.

H
...is for
HOLDINGS

If you have
one red stock,
two green,
and four blue,
they are your holdings,
the stocks that belong to you.

STOCK HOLDINGS

I

...is for

INVESTOR

When you buy a stock
or own an asset,
you're now an investor
and it's as
simple as that !

J

...is for

Joint VENTURE

When COMPANY-A and COMPANY-B
want to work together,
they shake hands,
become friends
and call it a Joint Venture !

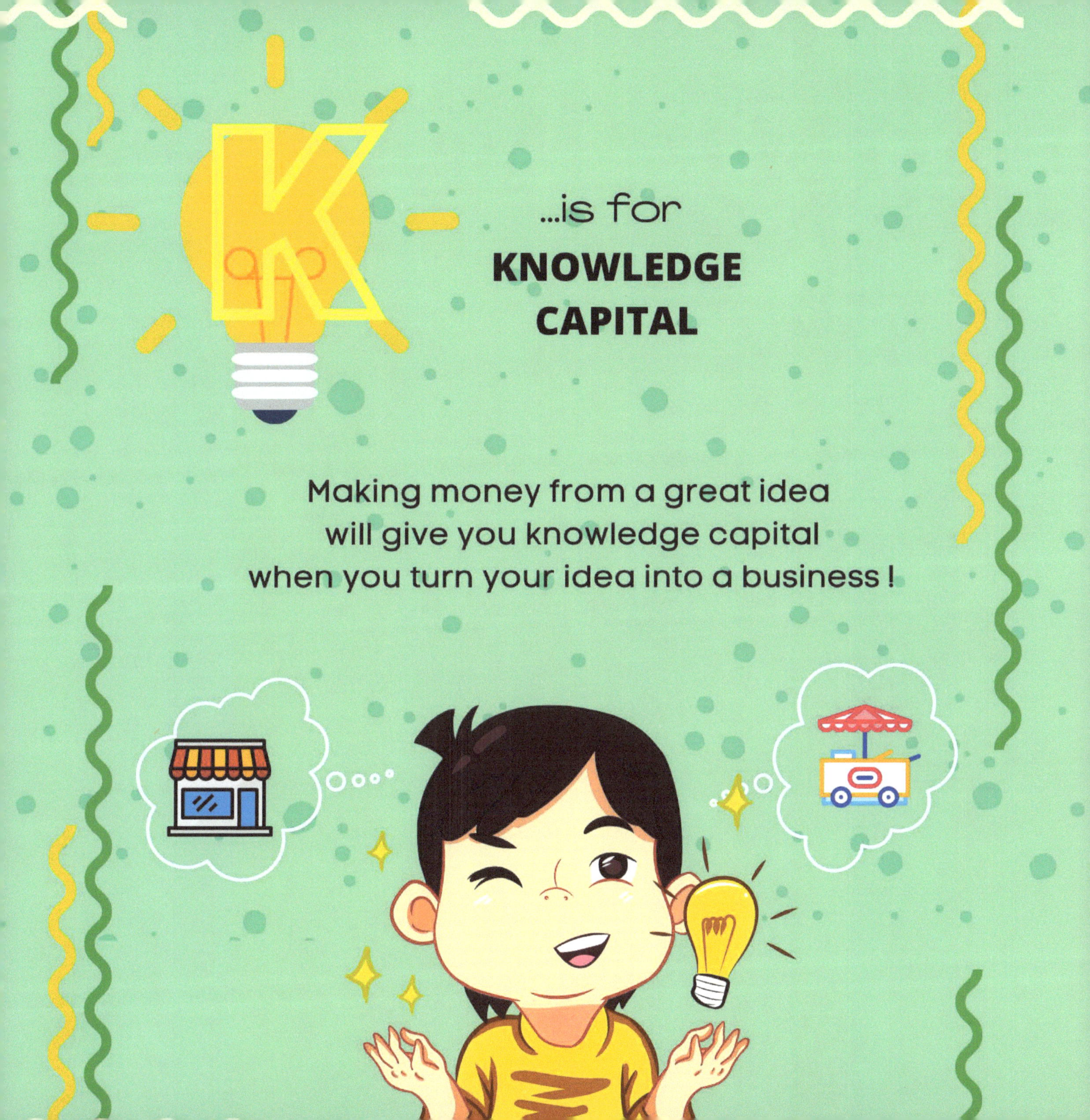
...is for
KNOWLEDGE
CAPITAL
Making money from a great idea
will give you knowledge capital
when you turn your idea into a business !

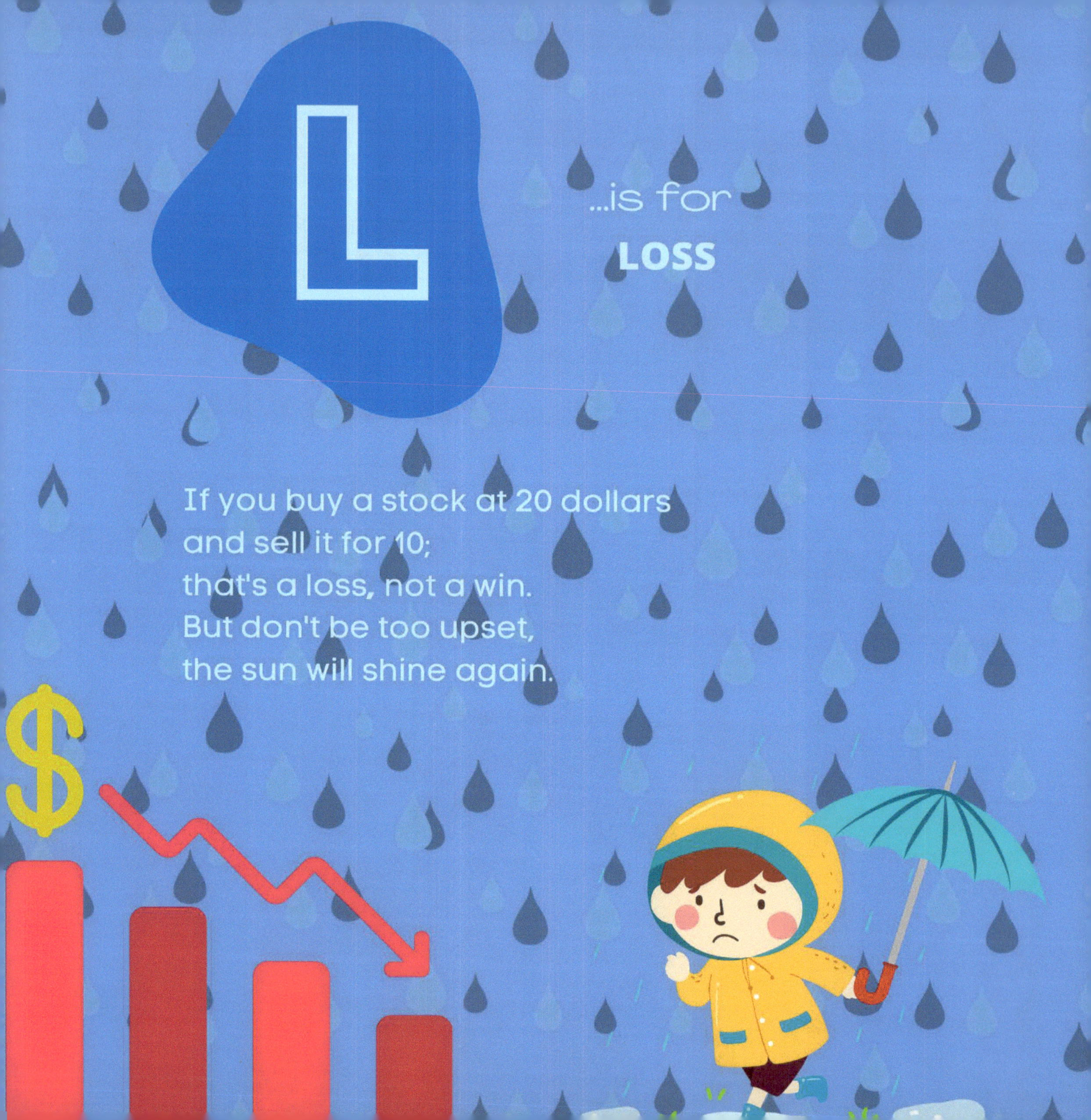

L
...is for
LOSS

If you buy a stock at 20 dollars
and sell it for 10;
that's a loss, not a win.
But don't be too upset,
the sun will shine again.

M
...is for
MARGIN

If you borrow money to buy a stock
you're investing with margin.
One day you will need to pay it back
even if your investment misses the target!

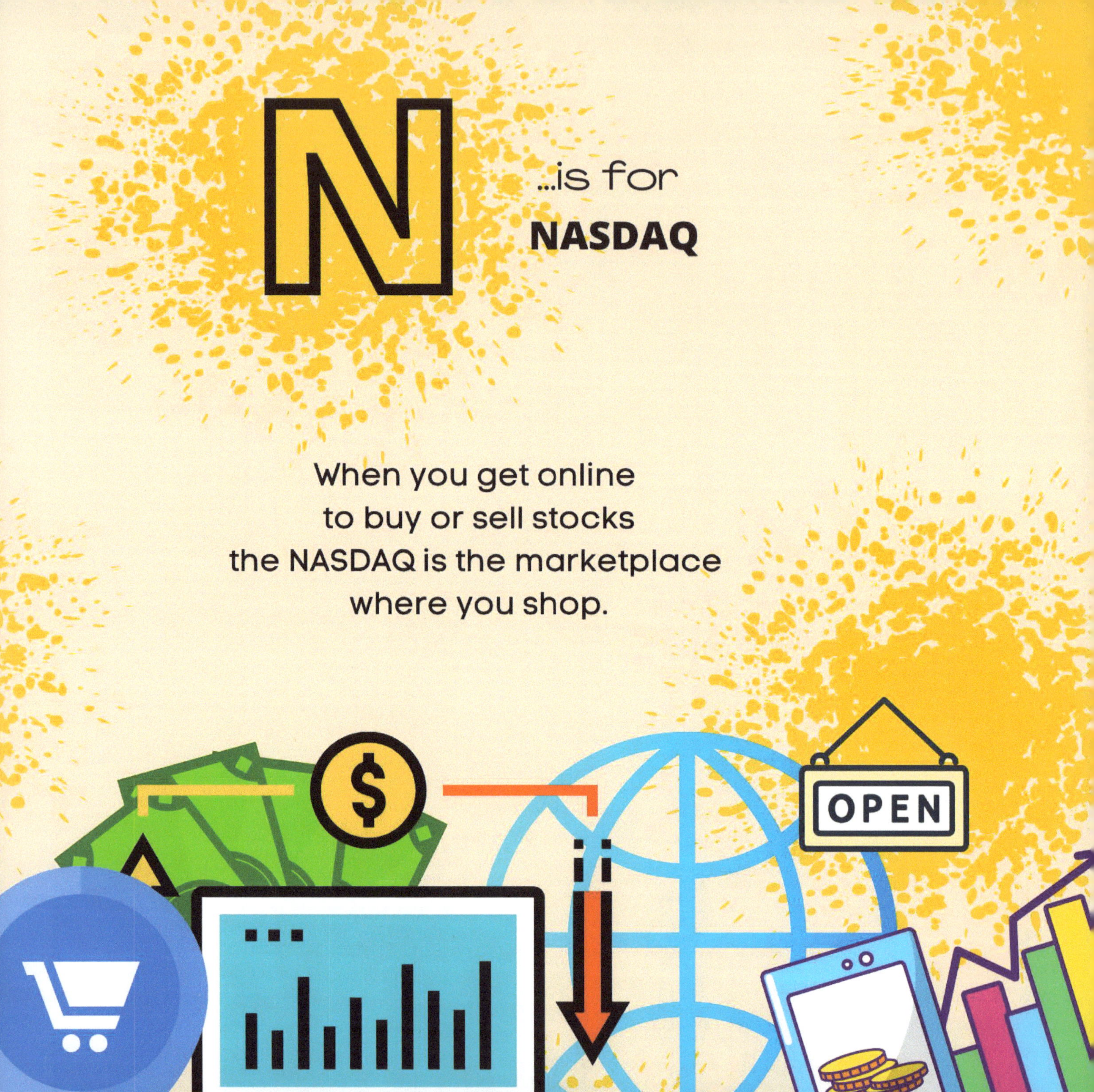

N
...is for
NASDAQ
When you get online
to buy or sell stocks
the NASDAQ is the marketplace
where you shop.
OPEN

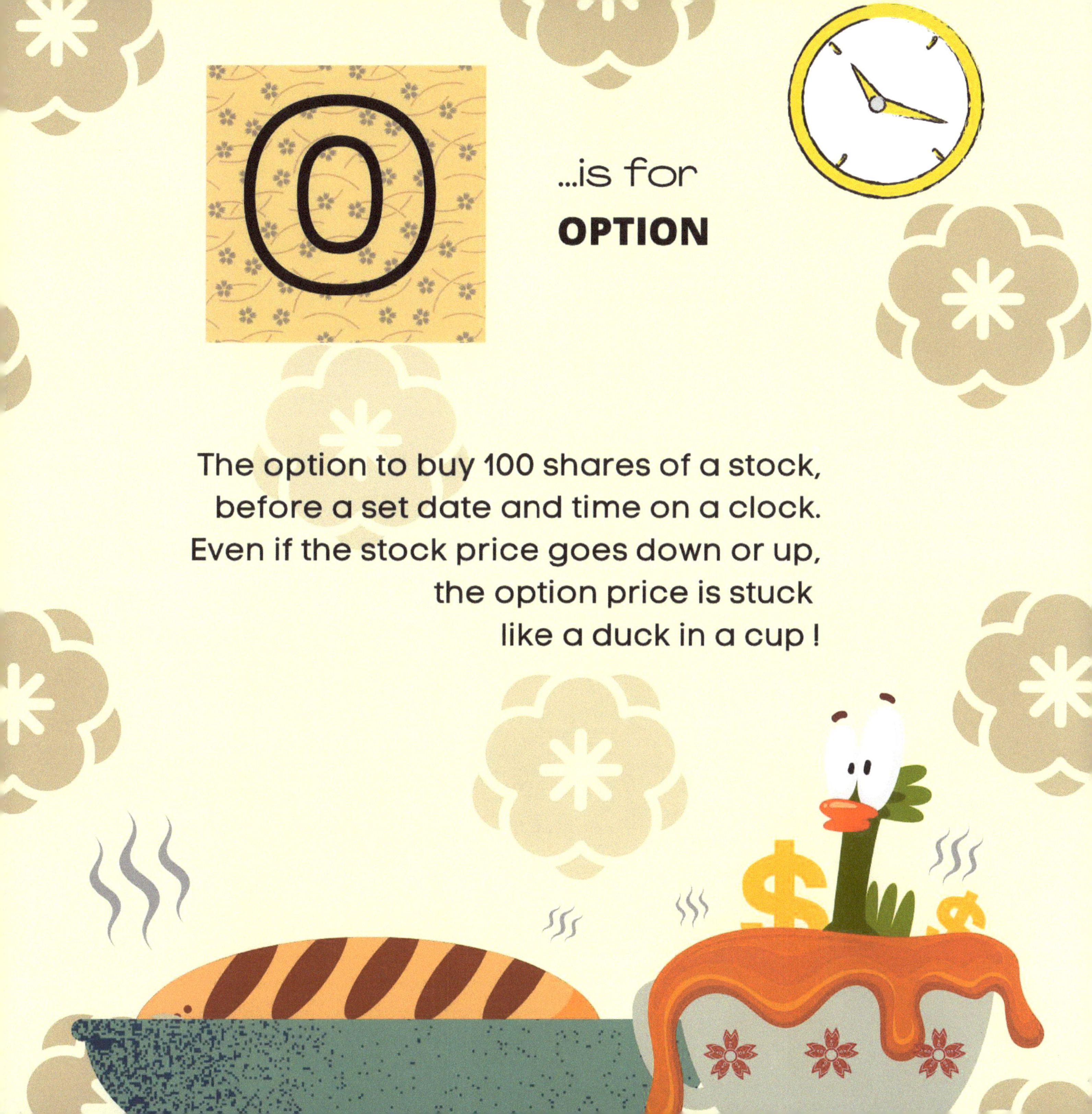

O

...is for OPTION

The option to buy 100 shares of a stock,
before a set date and time on a clock.
Even if the stock price goes down or up,
the option price is stuck
like a duck in a cup !

P

...is for

PUT

If you think the price will drop
like its really, really, hot.
Then buy a put option
and watch that stock price drop !

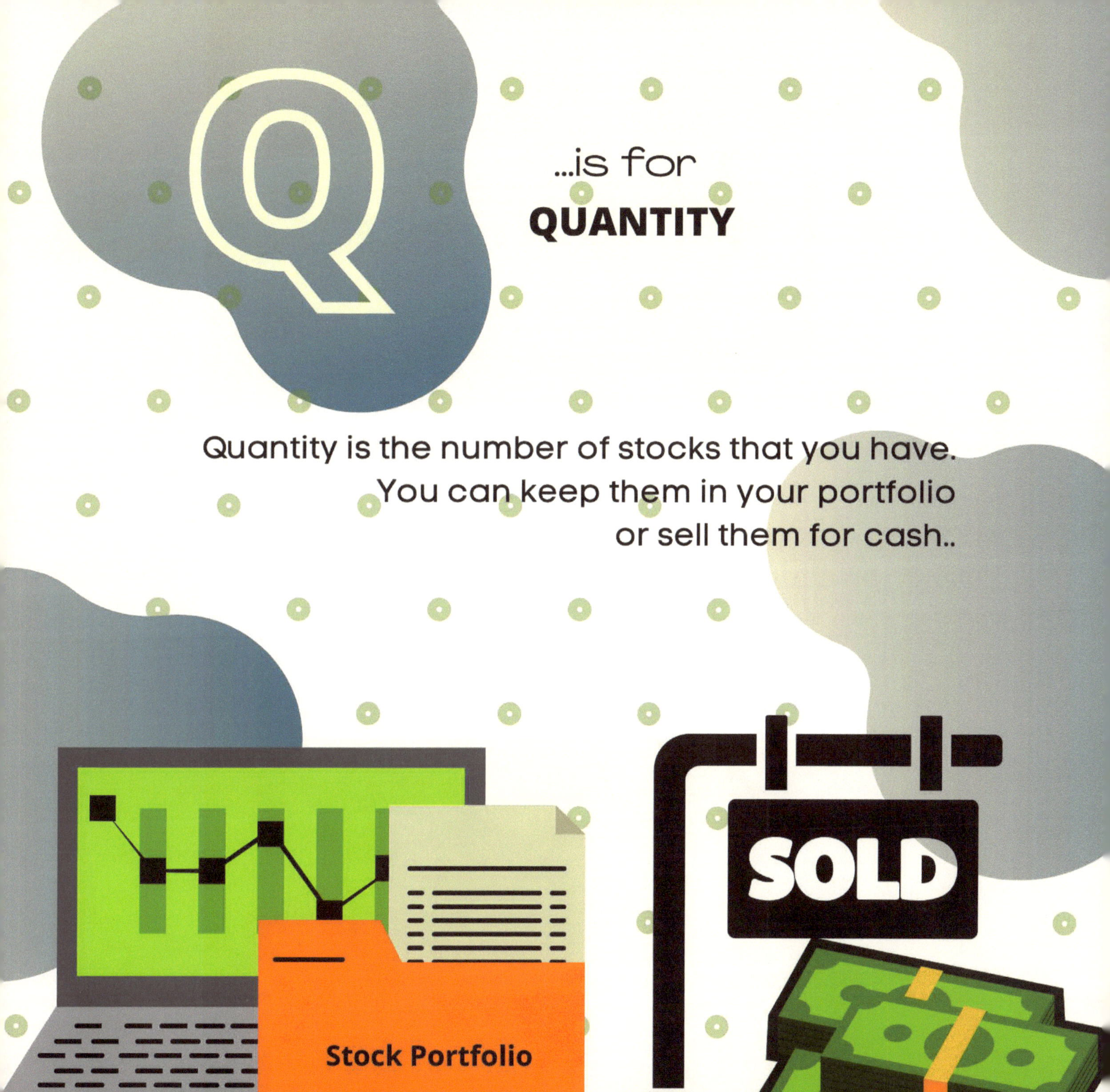
Q
...is for
QUANTITY
Quantity is the number of stocks that you have.
You can keep them in your portfolio
or sell them for cash..
Stock Portfolio
SOLD

R

...is for

REVENUE

Revenue is how much money a business makes, doing the things that a business does.
Knowing a company's revenue can tell you just how good their business was.

S

...is for
STOCK

When you buy stock in a company
you own a small piece of the pie.
You should buy a stock when the share
price is low and not high !

T
...is for
TICKER
SYMBOL
A ticker symbol is like
a nickname for a stock.
It helps you find a company fast
when your shopping for stocks
Store
Ticker Symbol: TSLA
Ticker Symbol: AMZ

...is for

UNDERVALUE

When a stock is selling
at a price lower than its worth,
it's trading undervalue.
This is a great time to
"load the boat" and wait for
those stocks to grow...grOW...GROW!

V
...is for

VALUE

Before you buy shares of a stock
stop and check its value.
There's a bunch to learn,
about a company or firm,
that the stock price just won't tell you.

W
...is for
WALL STREET
This is the street where stocks are sold.
You can shop here
Monday through Friday, 9:30 to 4.
NEW YORK CITY
ONE WAY
WALL St

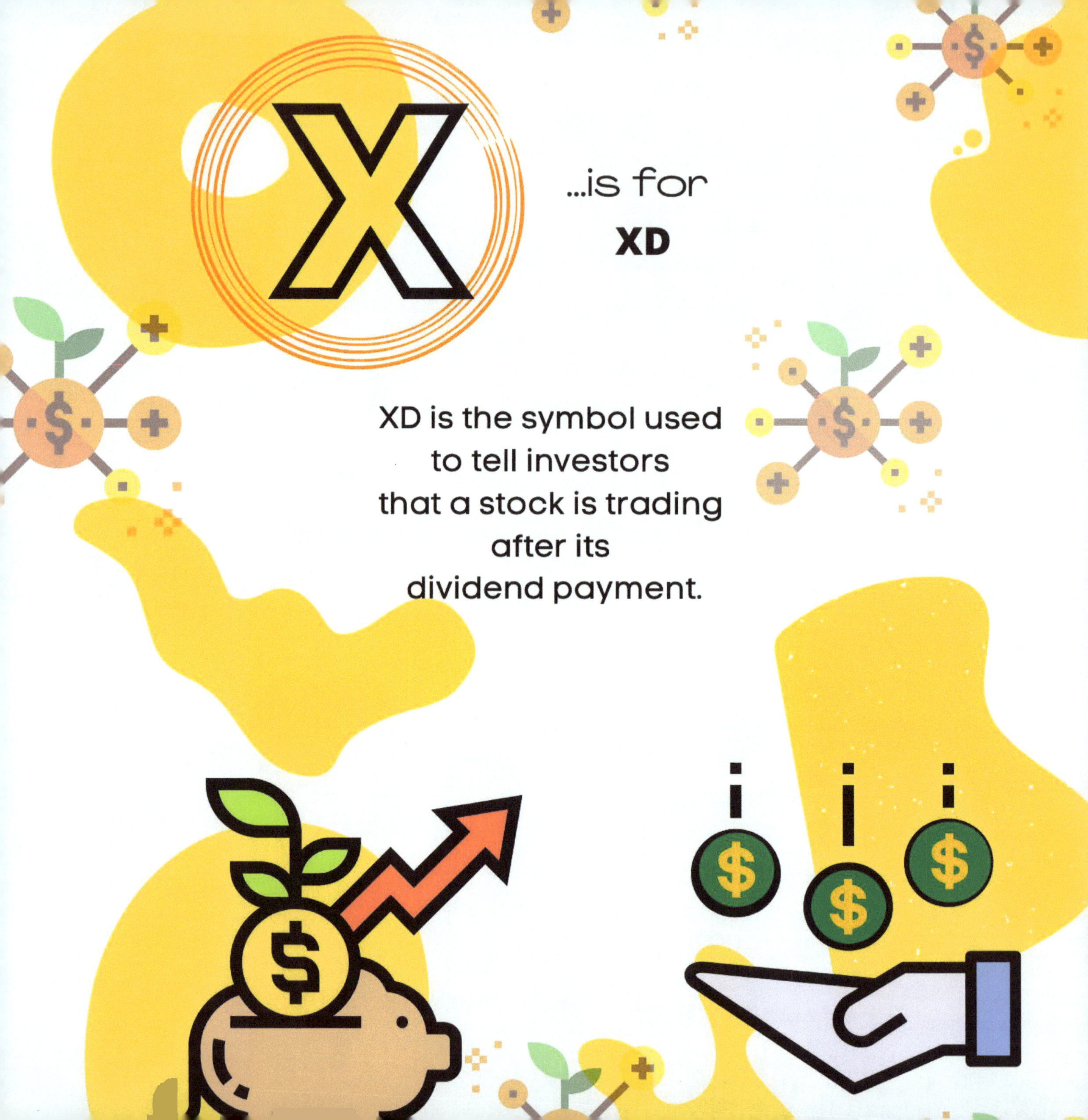

X
...is for
XD

XD is the symbol used
to tell investors
that a stock is trading
after its
dividend payment.

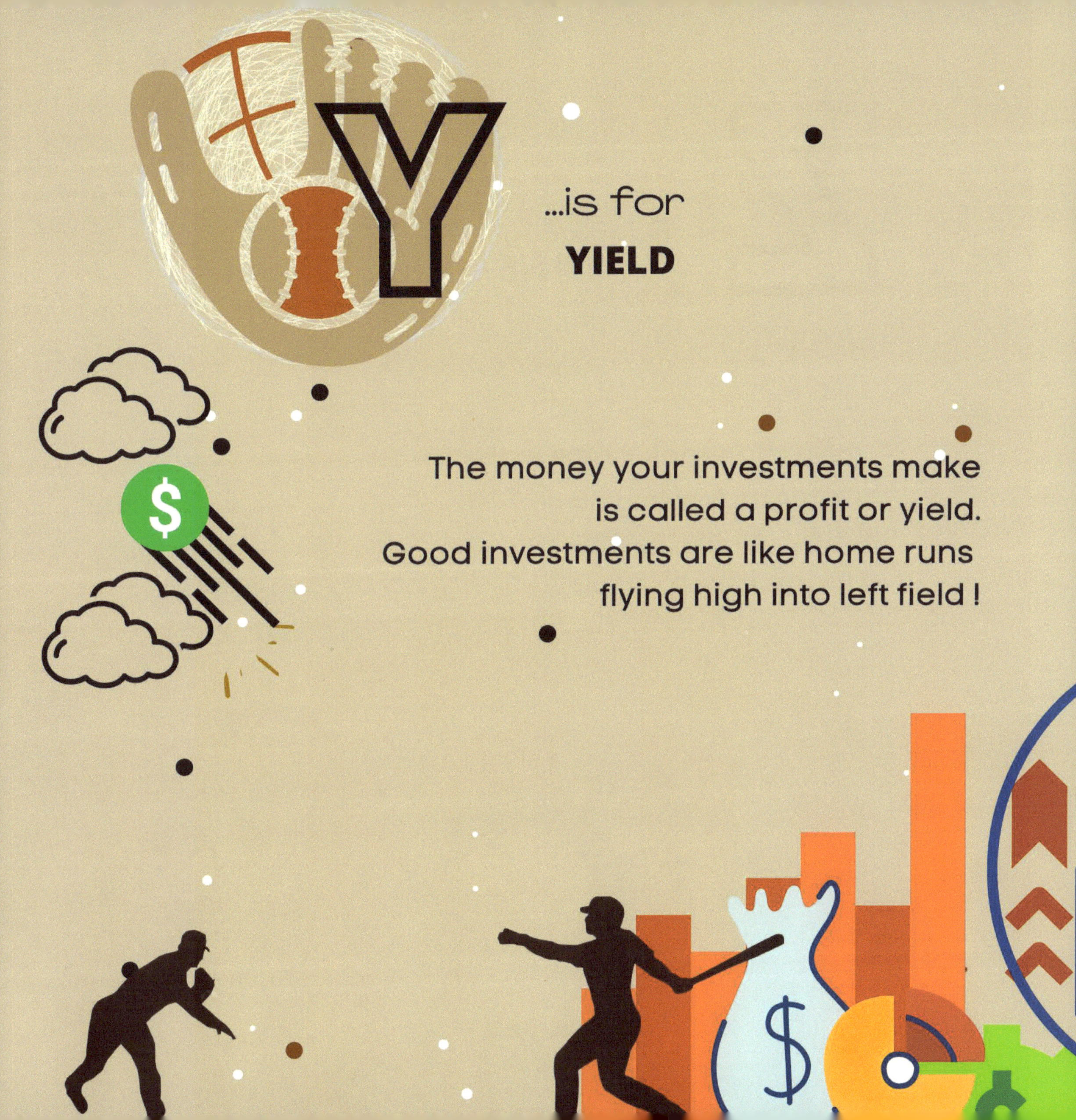
Y
...is for
YIELD

The money your investments make
is called a profit or yield.
Good investments are like home runs
flying high into left field !

Z

...is for

ZONE OF RESISTANCE

When the stock price is rising
higher than you predicted,
it may go even higher
if it can break through the zone of resistance.